Let's Learn About Literature

SONGS

Heather Moore Niver

Enslow Publishing
101 W. 23rd Street
Suite 240
New York, NY 10011
USA
enslow.com

Words to Know

accompany To play music along with a voice, a group, or another instrument.

by ear By listening to music.

chorus A large group of singers; a musical verse that is repeated.

ensemble A group of musicians, dancers, or actors who perform together.

jazz A kind of African American–inspired music. It is often made up on the spot, or improvised.

lyrics The words to a song.

melody A song's tune.

verse Lines of writing that have rhythm and sometimes rhyme.

work A piece of music or literature.

CONTENTS

Most children hear and sing songs from a young age.

Sing a Song

Do you have a favorite song? Songs are a kind of music. Many nursery rhymes are set to music. These are some of the first songs that kids learn.

Fast Fact

Lullabies like "Twinkle, Twinkle, Little Star" are songs that help put babies to sleep.

A man sings a song while many instruments play along.

One Voice

A song is a musical work. It has a **melody**. It is sung by a person, or voice. It may have an instrument **accompany** it.

Fast Fact

Music sung without any instruments is called *a capella.*

The Beatles were a famous quartet who became popular in the 1960s.

One, Two, Three, Four

One person singing a song is called a solo. Two voices singing together is a duet. A trio is when three voices sing together. Four voices form a quartet.

Fast Fact

Instruments can also play solos, duets, trios, and quartets.

The lyrics to this lullaby are written along with the musical notes.

Words and Music

Lyrics are the words in a song. They are paired with music to make a song. Music can give the words more power or emotion.

Fast Fact

Sometimes poems are set to music, like "Puff the Magic Dragon," by Leonard Lipton.

The chorus to "This Land Is Your Land":

This land is your land
This land is my land
From California to the New York island;
From the red wood forest to the Gulf Stream waters
This land was made for you and me.

Verse and Chorus

A song usually has **verses** to tell the story. Each verse is different. The **chorus** stays the same, like in the folk song "This Land Is Your Land."

Fast Fact

"Chorus" can also mean a large group of singers performing together.

This folk duo play a guitar and a banjo while they sing.

Folk Songs

One type of song is the folk song. Folk songs are usually simple tunes that have been passed down over many years. The guitar and banjo are sometimes played.

Fast Fact

In folk songs, music notes and words are not written down. They are learned by ear.

A singer performs an art song with piano accompaniment.

Art Songs

Art songs are more formal than folk songs. People who are trained singers usually perform them. They are performed with piano accompaniment or an **ensemble**.

Selena Gomez is one of today's most well-known pop singers.

Pop!

Popular songs are also known as "pop" songs. Pop songs can include lots of different styles. They often have a catchy tune and a chorus.

FAST FACT

"Yellow Submarine" by the Beatles is a pop song for kids—and adults!

Bobby McFerrin is known for imitating instruments using only his voice.

Making It Up

In some **jazz** songs the singer uses made-up words. They might scat, or make up the tune as they go along. Sometimes, the singer sounds like a musical instrument!

Fast Fact

Jazz singer Ella Fitzgerald sang the children's song "A-Tisket, A-Tasket."

Activity

Write Your Own Song!

MATERIALS

- notebook
- pencil

Maybe now you are thinking you would like to write your own song. Here are a few steps to get you started:

- Decide what you want the song to be about. Some ideas might be your favorite animal, a season or holiday that is

coming up, or something you just learned about in school.

- Next pick a melody. A great first step is to choose one you already know. It may be a good idea to use a simple one at first, like "Row, Row, Row, Your Boat."
- Now start thinking of what words go with your melody.
- Here's an example:

  Write, write, write your song,
  Easy as can be!
  When it's done, it will be fun
  If you will sing with me!

Learn More

Books

Ajmera, Maya, Elise Hofer Derstine, and Cynthia Pon. *Music Everywhere!* Watertown, MA: Charlesbridge, 2014.

Anderson, Steven. *Miss Mary Mack*. North Mankato, MN: Cantata Learning, 2016.

Hennenberg, Susan. *What Is a Song?* New York, NY: Britannica Educational Books, 2015.

Websites

Learn How to Write a Song: A Step-By-Step Guide
robinfrederick.com/learn-how-to-write-a-song/
Check out this step-by-step guide to writing a song.

Music Games
pbskids.org/games/music/
Learn more about music with these fun games!

Index

Published in 2019 by Enslow Publishing, LLC.
101 W. 23rd Street, Suite 240, New York, NY 10011

Library of Congress Cataloging-in-Publication Data

Names: Niver, Heather Moore, author.
Title: Songs / Heather Moore Niver.
Description: New York, NY : Enslow Publishing, 2019. | Series: Let's learn about literature | Includes bibliographical references and index. | Audience: Grades K-4.
Identifiers: LCCN 2017048844| ISBN 9780766097599 (library bound) | ISBN 9780766097605 (pbk.) | ISBN 9780766097612 (6 pack)
Subjects: LCSH: Songs—Analysis, appreciation—Juvenile literature. | Music appreciation—Juvenile literature.
Classification: LCC ML3928 .N58 2019 | DDC 782.42—dc23
LC record available at https://lccn.loc.gov/2017048844

Printed in the United States of America

Photo Credits: Cover, p. 1 Monkey Business Images/Shutterstock.com; pp. 2–3, 24 Gurza/Shutterstock.com; p. 4 SpeedKingz/Shutterstock.com; pp. 5, 7, 9, 11, 13, 15, 17, 19, 21, 22–23 (paper, notebook, pencil) narmacero/Shutterstock.com; pp. 5, 7, 11, 15, 17, 19, 21, 22 (open book) Wen Wen/Shutterstock.com; p. 6 Louai Beshara/AFP/Getty Images; p. 8 Michael Ochs Archives/Getty Images; p. 10 MusicImages/Alamy Stock Photo; p. 12 Bettmann/Getty Images; p. 14 Linda Vartoogian/Archive Photos/Getty Images; p. 16 Hiroyuki Ito/Hulton Archive/Getty Images; p. 18 Chris McKay/Getty Images; p. 20 Douglas Mason/Getty Images; p. 22 TCreativeMedia/Shutterstock.com.